Even God is *Single*

(so stop giving me a hard time).

by Karen Salmansohn

Illustrated by Ed Fotheringham. Designed by Liska + Associates.

Text copyright © 2000 Karen Salmansohn
Illustrations copyright © Ed Fotheringham
Design copyright © Liska + Associates

Library of Congress Cataloging-in-
Publication Data
Salmansohn, Karen.
    Even God is single : so stop giving
me a hard time / by Karen Salmansohn ;
illustrated by Ed Fotheringham.
      p. cm.
    ISBN 0-7611-2134-X
      1. Single women–Humor. I. Title

PN6231.S5485 S25 2000
305.48'9652'0207–dc21   00-042649

Concept and creative direction by
Karen Salmansohn
Illustrated by Ed Fotheringham
Designed by Liska + Associates

Workman books are available at special
discounts when purchased in bulk for
premiums and sales promotions as well
as for fund-raising or educational use.
Special editions or book excerpts can
also be created to specification. For
details, contact the Special Sales
director at the address below.

Workman Publishing Company, Inc.
708 Broadway
New York, NY 10003-9555

Printed in Hong Kong

First printing, October 2000
10 9 8 7 6 5 4 3 2 1

If you're a single woman, chances are you've been asked the following 3 questions...

1. Why aren't you **married?**

2. Why **aren't** you married?

...and the very, very popular:

3. Why aren't **you** married?

(give or take another 999,999,997 more such questions)

there are nearly as many answers. Happily, many even include **factors to blame other than yourself and/or your thighs.**

Unfortunately, I can't fix you up with any cute guys. However, I can fix you up with some **feisty comebacks** to fling at anyone who dares to question your single status.

And that's the purpose of this book—to remind you why you should feel good about your singlehood, so you can better defend yourself against anyone who tries to make you feel like **half of a person**, just because you're not

half of a couple.

Trust me. It's worth it to hold out for a **soulmate**

instead of a mere **cellmate** to share your life with.

This book will help to reassure you about your love-life choices during any and all times of inner turmoil—i.e. **those dreaded family visits** or nights **out with your nudgy married friends.** Speaking of the unenlightened, this book should be generously offered up to any and all of the above to help them enlighten up. Now, once again, for the question that inspired this book (after all, a single girl can never hear it—or even see it in print—enough times)...

After hearing that question, you will pause, smil

...gaciously (I love that word), and give one of the following...

6

good, snappy single-girl comebacks...

In the beginning, there were no stairmasters or low-fat-high-fiber muffins, and so people lived to only about 40-something. Maximum.

Meaning? The pressure was on to get married before age 25. However, today, thanks to medical advances—and the fine line of SnackWell products—we can all hope to live to age 80. Easy.

Meaning? Even if we get married at age 40, that's still 35, 45, even 55 years to be with a mate. Plenty of time to be married.

And divorced...

What's the hurry?

Married people are not necessarily better catches simply because they were caught. I mean, have you taken a look at some of the married people out there?

Hitler got married. **Frankenstein got married.** Linda Tripp got married. Obviously married people are not superior people...

Meanwhile, look at some of our cool single role models: **Catwoman: single.**

Buddha: single. Aphrodite: single. Madonna. The Lone Ranger. Actually, all superheroes are single: Superman, Wonder Woman, Dudley Do-Right, etc.

Then there's The Ultimate Superhero...**God.** Also

4

single. And God is even a single-parent household.

It's easy to become married. 2.3 million people do it a year. If you want to pressure me to become something, hey, why not pick something a little more challenging—

like an **astrophysicist.**

Why am I single?...

It's a mystery right up there with: **Who Shot JFK?**

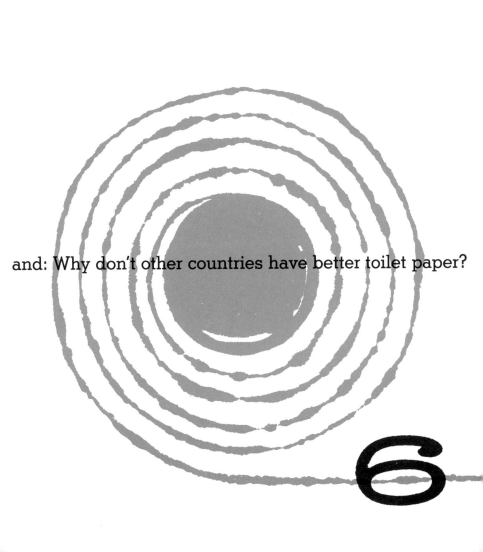

and: Why don't other countries have better toilet paper?

6

7
The best things in life are **free...**

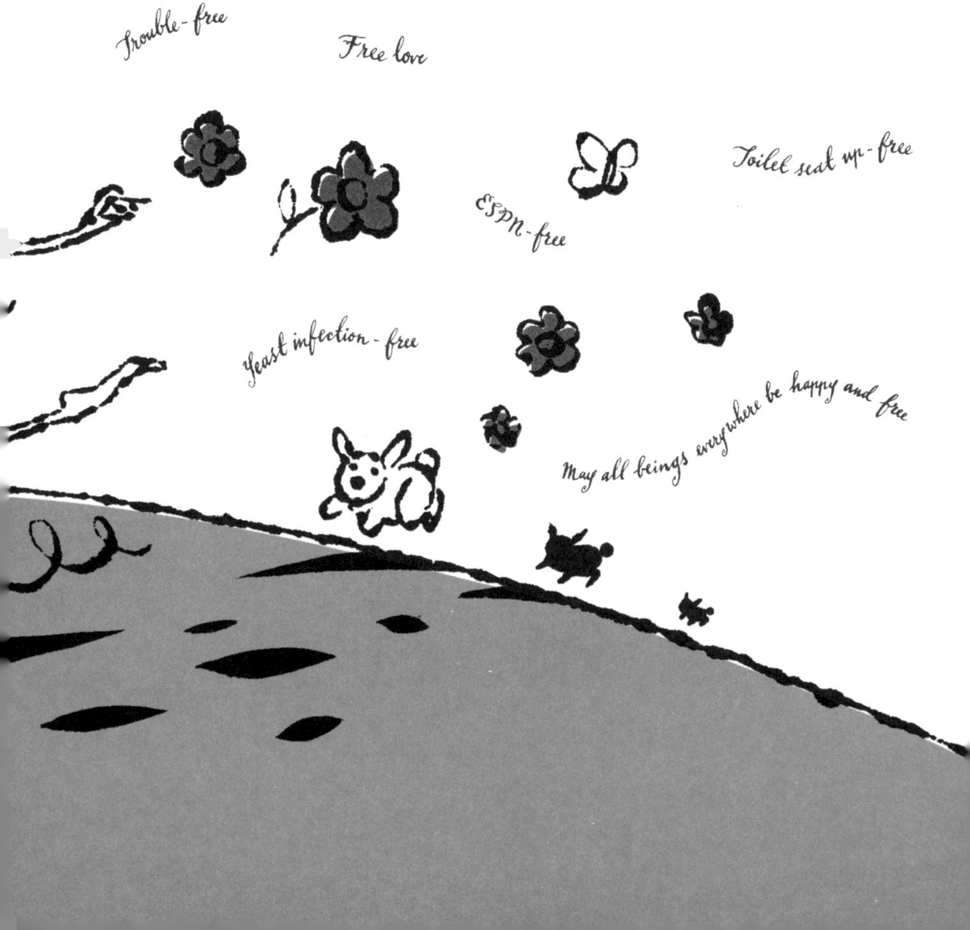

Trouble-free

Free love

Toilet seat up-free

ESPN-free

Yeast infection-free

May all beings everywhere be happy and free

Why limit myself to being dissatisfied by one relationship.

As Granma Nan says,

"Why make one man happy, when you
can make a lot of men happy?"

8

when I can be dissatisfied by **an infinite variety?**

Many fabulous things don't necessarily come in pairs. For instance, there's **only one**
Hope Diamond.

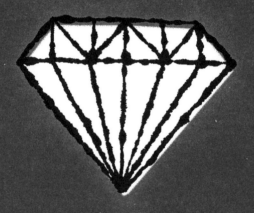

Why settle when hope springs eternal?

Consider the following verbal similarities, then

Bridal vs

ask yourself: **coincidence or what?**

Altar vs. Altered

Settling Down vs. Settling

I Do vs. Child Support Due

Married vs. Marred

Bridled

Wedded vs. Welded

Mate vs. Inmate

Wedding vs. Weeding

Engaged vs. Enraged

Monogamy vs. Monotony

In-laws vs. Outlaws

Wedlock vs. Deadlock

Committed vs. "Committed" (you know, that other kind...Oh, and also consider how marriage is called "An institution." ahem.)

10

Marriage vs. Mirage

I Do vs. I Guess You Will Do

One of a

Singular

Singled Out.

Now, consider all the cool vocabulary related
to non-marrieds:

kind.
Single-most.

Saving the best for last.

ensation.

A hit single.

Good things **do** come to those who wait.

11

which reminds me...

Plus, I suppose it helps that wit▸

According to the U.S. Census Bureau, **good things do come to those who wait.** Statistics show that creased age comes

• • • • • • • • • • • • • • • • •

creased eyesight and increased memory loss.

Both marital aids.

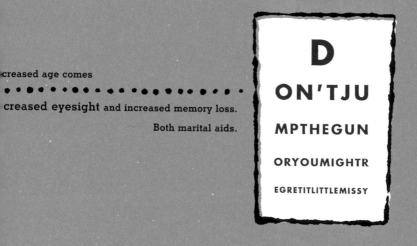

D

ON'TJU

MPTHEGUN

ORYOUMIGHTR

EGRETITLITTLEMISSY

12

folks who **wait until their 30s to marry** experience a much lower divorce rate. Probably because we're older and wider—oops, I meant wiser.

DRIVER'S L[ICENSE]

WEIGHT:
NONE OF YOUR BUSINESS

HAIR:
BRUNETTE, SOMETIMES RED, ONCE FUCHSI[A]

AGE:
YOUNGISH

HEIGHT:
IN PRADA? BIRKENSTOCKS?

Why rush to get married by a specific age, when

13

it's much simpler to just **lie about one's age?**

14

Thanks to modern day science, **biological clocks**

Meaning?

are now available with a **snooze-button option.**

We have more time to shop for the ultimate husband.

Returns

15

Consider the statistics: **Over 50% of marrieds undo their "I dos".** The way I see it, being careful about whom I marry just means I've...

(Marriage must be a really great thing.
Some people seem to like it so much,
they do it 2, 3, even 8 times in a lifetime.)

skipped a few divorces.

16 While I'm shining the harsh light of truth on the make-up-smudged face of marriage, let me remind you that **longevity in wedlock does not necessarily mean a lifetime of bliss and satisfaction, either.** So, why is marriage made out to be this big Holy Grail? I blame fairy tales. They're false advertising for happily-ever-after marriagehood. You know what I'd love to see? The sequel to Snow White...

It's interesting how our culture has the expression **"happily married,"** but no expression **"happily single."** And those words are 100% U.S. Census Bureau Certified. Statistics show that although married men are reported to be happier than single men —**single women are reported to be happier than married**

"Lately I've been feeling like he's got some screws loose..."

women—a fact that only furthers the irony that single women are branded as "Unhappy" and "Lonely" and "Loser-esque"—when single women are just boldly holding out for the **right situation,** rather than in a weakened state of desperation getting married just to get married—only to wind up feeling "Unhappy" and "Lonely" and "Loser-esque" within their marriage—until divorce do them part...

"Why settle for Mr. Good Enough
or Mr. Rightish?"

18 Married people have their share of problems—as much as single people do. So, choosing to get

married girl problems...

married or remain single is simply a matter of
deciding which kind of problems you want to have:

or **single girl** problems.

Like **that** woman's husband...

or <u>**that**</u> woman's husband!

19

"*Je ne regrette*

As Edith Piaf, the French chanteuse, once belted out: "Je ne regrette rien, j'avance." Which translated into Single Girl English means:

"...rien, j'avance"

"Hey, I don't regret a darn thing about my dating life. I'm learning lots—plus, I'm getting some really **swell jewelry**."

I'm trendy. According to the U.S. Census Bureau, marriage rates are **plummeting downwards...**

21 while single rates are rising upwards, increasingly so every year. Who knows, eventually traditional marriage could be the **beta tape of love unions.**

There's less of a need for marriage now than there was **centuries (or even decades) ago**, when marriage represented financial rescue for a woman. Now I, as a modern day broad, can gain:

money

influence

identity

status

and stability

all on my own—and not through a man.

Meaning? I now have the freedom to hold out for **a spouse who will be more than a walking wallet,** but a best friend who knows how to find both my G-spot and the baby's diaper bag.

Meaning, it's a case of:

I think, therefore... I am single.

IN·CHRG

22

It's a case of
"Smart Women, No Choices."

BOSS

23

Many women are overqualified for the job of wife, because most men are not looking for a woman with **"CEO-level wife skills."** Meaning, if you are too independent, or want to create your own hours, or seek emotional raises, then there won't be as many openings for the kind of wife position you are seeking. Two big problems with relationships today:
1. There is no room for two husbands.

2. Most women need a wife.

There're **too many potential partners** to choose from. As long as George Clooney, John Cusack, and Ben Affleck are still single, what's the rush?

GEORGE

JOHN

BEN

Ironically, we singles now have the largest love buffet of any era. We can date someone 20 years younger or older, of a different color/race/religion—or even region, thanks to planes, trains, and e-mail. Unfortunately, it seems more choices mean more bonding problems. For instance, now that the Soviets have more freedom, they're catching up to us in divorce.

There's a **limited selection of potential partners.** All the really sexy, sensitive, stylish, just-plain-swell guys already have boyfriends.

BRUCE + SID

Answer me this: why when we are younger do our mothers never think any guy is good enough? But as we get older, we could wheel in a guy in a coma, announce our engagement, and our mothers would do wheelies for joy.

24

Okay, so maybe **I haven't yet found "thee" one yet,** but **I have found plenty of "a" one's**—all of whom have helped to make me become a wiser,

(for a good time close and open

25

more honest, more soulful, more communicative partner for the next relationship—as well as better in bed—which also helps a lot in relationships, believe me.

and open book, close and open book)

In summary, I say: let's stop pressuring women to marry for the sake of marriage. Instead, I say: let's start pressuring **people**—both women and men people—to strive to become wiser, more communicative, more honest, more

soulful, and more sexually talented people—and thereby increase the potential field of better, happier marital partners to pick from—and/or simply increase the potential field of

just better,

happier people.

the end

(of the single girl vs. married girl debate)